God Is Love

GOD is Love

REFLECTIONS
ON HIS INSPIRING PRESENCE
IN OUR DAILY LIVES

HALLMARK EDITIONS

ACKNOWLEDGMENTS: I Corinthians 13; Proverbs 31:11-13, 26-28; Ruth 1:16-17; and I John 4:7-13 from the *King James Version Bible*. Reprinted by permission of the Cambridge University Press. Published by the Syndics of Cambridge University Press. "Of Marriage" from *A Second Treasury of Kahlil Gibran*. Copyright © 1962 by The Citadel Press, Secaucus, N.J. Reprinted with permission. "Revealer of Truth" from *A New Song* by Pat Boone. © 1970 by Charles Eugene Boone. Reprinted with permission of the publisher, Creation House. "After Two Years" from *The Poems of Richard Aldington*. Copyright 1928, 1930, 1933, 1934 by Doubleday & Company, Inc. Reprinted with permission. "Brothers" by Randy Phillips, from *Ebony Jr!*, August/September 1973. Reprinted by permission of *Ebony Jr!* Copyright, 1973 by Johnson Publishing Company, Inc. Excerpt by Billy Graham. © Billy Graham. Reprinted with permission. "A Child's Wisdom" by Lorna Beall reprinted by permission from *Guideposts Magazine*. Copyright 1974 by Guideposts Associates, Inc., Carmel, New York 10512. "Love's Source" excerpt from p. 107 from *In Holy Marriage* by George E. Sweazey. Copyright © 1966 by George E. Sweazey. Reprinted by permission of Harper & Row, Publishers, Inc. "The Basic Passion" from *Three to Get Married* by Fulton J. Sheen. Copyright, 1951, by Fulton J. Sheen. Reprinted by permission of Hawthorn Books, Inc. "A Family Prayer" from *The Prayers of Peter Marshall*, edited by Catherine Marshall. Copyright 1954 by Catherine Marshall. Used with permission of McGraw-Hill Book Company. "The God of Love" from *The World as I See It* by Albert Schweitzer. Reprinted by permission of the Philosophical Library, Inc. Excerpt by Joe E. Wells © 1953 by The New York Times Company. Reprinted by permission. "God Blessed Our Marriage" from *Mine Eyes Have Seen the Glory* by Anita Bryant. Copyright © 1970 by Fleming H. Revell Company. Used by permission. "Afsana-Sisana" from *UNICEF Book of Children's Poems* by William Kaufman, published by Stackpole Books. Reprinted with permission. "Transformation" by Pauline Havard from *Unity*, December 1974. "A Closer Walk" by Mary Jane Henderson from *Unity*, November 1974. "I Am Loved!" by Mary Rowe from *Unity*, January 1974. "What God Is Like" from *What God Is Like* by James Dillet Freeman. Published by Unity Books. © 1973. All reprinted by permission of Unity Books. Excerpt reprinted by permission of Schocken Books, Inc. from *On Judaism* by Martin Buber. Copyright © 1967 by Schocken Books, Inc.

A Gift From God

True love's the gift which God has given
To man alone beneath the heaven...
It is the secret sympathy,
The silver link, the silken tie,
Which, heart to heart and mind to mind,
In body and in soul can bind.

Sir Walter Scott

Thank God for Life

Let my voice ring out and over the earth,
Through all the grief and strife,
With a golden joy in a silver mirth:
Thank God for life!

Let my voice swell out through the great abyss
To the azure dome above,
With a chord of faith in the harp of bliss:
Thank God for Love!

Let my voice thrill out beneath and above,
The whole world through:
O my Love and Life, O my Life and Love,
Thank God for you!

James Thomson

To Grow in Love

I believe in God, who is for me spirit, love, the principle of all things. I believe that God is in me, as I am in Him. I believe that the true welfare of man consists in fulfilling the will of God. I believe that from the fulfillment of the will of God there can follow nothing but that which is good for me and for all men. I believe that the will of God is that every man should love his fellowmen, and should act toward others as he desires that they should act toward him. I believe that the reason of life is for each of us simply to grow in love. I believe that this growth in love will contribute more than any other force to establish the Kingdom of God on earth. To replace a social life in which division, falsehood and violence are all-powerful with a new order in which humanity, truth and brotherhood will reign.

Leo Tolstoy

Love is an image of God, and not a lifeless image nor one painted on paper, but the living essence of the Divine Nature, which beams full of all goodness.

Martin Luther

God's Love

Beloved, let us love one another: for love is of God; and every one that loveth is born of God, and knoweth God.

He that loveth not knoweth not God; for God is love.

In this was manifested the love of God toward us, because that God sent his only begotten Son into the world, that we might live through him.

Herein is love, not that we loved God, but that he loved us, and sent his Son to be the propitiation for our sins.

Beloved, if God so loved us, we ought also to love one another.

No man hath seen God at any time. If we love one another, God dwelleth in us, and his love is perfected in us.

Hereby know we that we dwell in him, and he in us, because he hath given us of his Spirit.

I John 4:7-13

Of all the music that reaches farthest into heaven, it is the beating of a loving heart.

Henry Ward Beecher

What God Is Like

I did not know what God is like
Until a friendly word
Came to me in an hour of need—
And it was God I heard.

I did not know what God is like
Until I heard love's feet
On errands of God's mercy
Go up and down life's street.

I did not know what God is like
Until I felt a hand
Clasp mine and lift me when alone
I had no strength to stand.

I think I know what God is like,
For I have seen the face
Of God's son looking at me
From all the human race.

James Dillet Freeman

God Blessed Our Marriage

As the day of her wedding approached, entertainer Anita Bryant became aware of a potential problem in the marriage.

Time moved closer to June 25, the date Bob and I had set for our wedding. We both were so busy, so separated from one another, and still there remained one vitally important issue for us to settle.

The fact was: Bob and I had not talked sufficiently about our religious faith. He knew about mine, of course, and I knew he understood and approved of the place I reserve for God in my life.

But what about Bob? Like many other Swedes, he had been reared in the Lutheran denomination, which I greatly respect. But Bob had not been saved; he frankly admitted to being just a nominal Christian, and even looked somewhat puzzled when I tried to explain what I meant by being saved through Christ.

Had God not stepped in and taken over, this could have been a terribly dangerous place in our relationship. As our wedding approached, I became more and more serious. Bob, always sensitive to what is happening inside me, could see that I was in the process of turning everything about our forthcoming life over to the Lord, for His blessing and protection.

Bob sensed the solemnity of this thing. The night before our wedding, we went to see our minister and then we talked with Gloria Roe, my close friend in Christ....

I'll never forget the closeness among us as we knelt and asked God to bless our marriage. In a true sense, that commitment felt as deep and important as the actual ceremony to come.

As we talked—as Gloria gently drew Bob out about his Christian beliefs—something wonderful happened. The Spirit of God descended upon us. Bob felt led to confess Jesus Christ as his Lord and Saviour.

This came as the holiest, most amazing gift to our impending marriage. The radiance of that moment lingered through those final hours before our wedding and started our life together in perfect joy.

. . .

No one could tell me where my soul might be;
I searched for God, and He eluded me;
I sought my brother out and found all three.
                                    Ernest Crosby

After Two Years

She is all so slight
And tender and white
As a May morning.
She walks without hood
At dusk. It is good
To hear her sing.

It is God's will
That I shall love her still
As He loves Mary,
And night and day
I will go forth to pray
That she love me.

Richard Aldington

I Am Loved!

Writer Mary Rowe discusses the importance of loving ourselves in order to be channels of God's love.

Several years ago a jeweler came up with the idea of inscribing three short words on various items of jewelry: "I am loved." That is all. But the idea caught on—swept the city, in fact. Everywhere one went, one found friends wearing cuff links, or earrings, or pendants, or carrying money clips. Each one was showing confidence in the fact he or she was loved. It seems the time has come when many men and women are no longer afraid to proclaim this truth....

If we do not love ourself, to a degree at least, it is impossible for us to believe that others love us. We shrug off such declarations. We say: "You don't really mean it. You're just being kind." But why should we doubt them? We doubt them because we haven't learned to accept ourself as a lovable being....

We owe it to ourself and to God to love ourself—not in a narcissistic way, but in a Christ way. We owe it to ourself and to God to acknowledge we are truly made in the image and after the likeness of the King of love, and that therefore we are eminently lovable— every last one of us! And when we can love ourself as we should, then can we truly be channels of God's love to all the world.

Happiness

God sends children for another purpose than merely to keep up the race—to enlarge our hearts; to make us unselfish and full of kindly sympathies and affections; to give our souls higher aims; to call out all our faculties to extended enterprise and exertion and to bring round our firesides bright faces, happy smiles, and loving, tender hearts. — My soul blesses the great Father, every day, that He has gladdened the earth with little children.

Mary Howitt

The love which binds a family together
is a miraculous blessing
sent from God to give us happiness
and to help us
recognize our kinship
with all the world.

Billy Graham

The Basic Passion

Love is the basic passion of man. Every emotion of the heart is reducible to it. Without love we would never become better, for love is the impetus to perfection, the fulfillment of what we have not....

Love is an inclination or a tendency to seek what seems good. The lover seeks union with the good which is loved in order to be perfected by it. The mystery of all love is that it actually precedes every act of choice; one chooses because he loves, he does not love because he chooses. As St. Thomas put it, "All other passions and appetites presuppose love as their first root."

Fulton J. Sheen

The Greatest of These

Though I speak with the tongues of men and of angels, and have not love, I am become as sounding brass, or a tinkling cymbal. And though I have the gift of prophecy, and understand all mysteries, and all knowledge; and though I have all faith, so that I could remove mountains, and have not love, I am nothing. And though I bestow all my goods to feed the poor, and though I give my body to be burned, and have not love, it profiteth me nothing. Love suffereth long, and is kind; love envieth not; love vaunteth not itself, is not puffed up, Doth not behave itself unseemly, seeketh not her own, is not easily provoked, thinketh no evil; Rejoiceth not in iniquity, but rejoiceth in the truth; Beareth all things, believeth all things, hopeth all things, endureth all things. Love never faileth: but whether there be prophecies, they shall fail; whether there be tongues, they shall cease; whether there be knowledge, it shall vanish away. For we know in part, and we prophesy in part. But when that which is perfect is come, then that which is in part shall be done away. When I was a child, I spake as a child, I understood as a child, I thought as a child: but when I became a man, I put away childish things. For now we see through a glass, darkly; but then face to face: now I know in part; but then shall I know even as also I am known. And now abideth faith, hope, love, these three; but the greatest of these is love.

I Corinthians 13

Prayer for a Happy Marriage

Father in Heaven, may the joy that fills the hearts of this bride and groom today live with them always.

Grant them the gifts of understanding, consideration, gentleness and wisdom. May they be sweethearts, helpmates and friends through life's glad and sad times.

Make their home a good and happy place, filled with contentment for them, their family and friends.

Be with this joyful couple now as they begin their new life together and stay with them always, guarding and guiding them with your love.

Amen.

Love

Yes, Love is indeed a light from Heaven,
A spark of that immortal fire
With angels shared, by Allah given,
To live from earth our low desire.
Devotion wafts the soul above
But Heaven itself descends in Love.
A feeling from the Godhead caught,
To wean from self each sordid thought!
A ray of Him who formed the whole;
A glory circling round the soul.

Lord Byron

The Jewish Mother

Jewish custom bids the Jewish mother, after her preparations for the Sabbath have been completed on Friday evening, kindle the Sabbath lamp. That is symbolic of the Jewish woman's influence on her own home, and through it upon larger circles. She is the inspirer of a pure family life whose hallowing influences are incalculable; she is the center of all spiritual endeavors, the confidante and fosterer of every undertaking. To her the Talmudic sentence applies: "It is woman alone through whom God's blessings are vouchsafed to a house."

Henrietta Szold

Lo, soul! seest thou not God's purpose from
     the first?
The earth to be spann'd, connected by
     network,
The people to become brothers and sisters,
The races, neighbors, to marry and be given
     in marriage,
The oceans to be cross'd, the distant brought
     near,
The lands to be welded together.

Walt Whitman

Love's Source

The marriage service leaves us looking out along a road that leads on to endless joy. There will be hardships along that road, and disappointments. To travel it will require strong disciplines and intelligently worked-out ways. Much that is ahead is uncertain, but some things can be depended on as absolutely sure. "Faith, hope, love abide, these three; but the greatest of these is love."

The bride and groom can set forth with high hearts because they have faith in each other which is founded on their faith in God. They can face the future full of hope because they know what will bring their marriage its daily comforts and ultimate success. Side by side they can start down across the years held to each other by a love whose source is in the heart of God.

George E. Sweazey

Was there ever a grandparent, bushed after a day of minding noisy youngsters, who hasn't felt the Lord knew what He was doing when He gave little children to young people?

Joe E. Wells

23

Nuptial Prayer

O God of wisdom, who has said
   Man should not walk alone
Be with us now who choose to tread
   Together, as Thine own.

As we before thine altar fair
   Repeat the sacred vow,
To keep it make us now aware
   That Thou must show us how.

Be near when dark clouds roll our way
   And from temptations, free;
But when we walk through sunny days
   Make us remember Thee.

And most of all keep our faith strong,
   May it our lives enshrine;
That this love may our whole life long
   Be like to that divine.

Charlotte Carpenter

Revealer of Truth

In his book "A New Song," *popular entertainer Pat Boone describes his wife Shirley's discovery of God's love through the power of the Holy Spirit.*

As she's often said since then, the whole world didn't suddenly become beautiful. But now, for the first time in many months, Shirley discovered that God was as near as her own heartbeat when she needed help. She stumbled many times, but whenever she did, she found Him ready to lift her up and encourage her along the way.

Also for the first time in many months, she began to read the Bible for a better understanding of the Lord. She was confident that she knew God, the Father. She was also certain that she knew God the Son, Jesus Christ, because she had accepted Him as her Savior and her Lord. But she did not know God the Holy Spirit. Lately she'd heard me talk about Him, and she had met a few people who talked about His presence as a reality, as a guide and counselor in the everyday problems of life.

As she read the Word of God, she began to see that the Holy Spirit was as personal as

God and Jesus Christ. Jesus talked about Him as the *revealer of truth.* So she prayed that she might understand all that this truth should mean to her. She also began to borrow the Bible tapes, and use them in the stereo in *her* car, as I was now doing.

What she came to learn is the beautiful fact that *when you know the Holy Spirit,* He gives you a love for people that you can't understand or explain yourself! And of course, this was what was about to happen in our family relationship. As the Bible plainly says in Romans 5:5, "...because the love of God has been poured out within our hearts through the Holy Spirit who was given to us."

Like all of us, Shirley had to learn that she must first love God *above everything else.* That's the Universal Key—the unconditional opening of the door. When that happened, then He could open her eyes and heart and mind to the fullness of the Holy Spirit, so that His love would then be "poured out" in her heart for those about her.

. . .

Look down and bless them from above
And keep their hearts alight with love.
Robert Hugh Benson

Afsana-Sisana

Afsana - Sisana
Forty birds clamor...
I cooked a very good stew
And ate it so nobody knew.
I gave some to a farmer to eat;
The farmer gave me some wheat.
I took the wheat to a mill;
They gave me flour, my fill.
With flour to a taghaar I went;
The taghaar gave me some ferment.
The ferment I gave to a baker;
He gave me a loaf, the bread-maker.
To a shepherd I gave the bread;
He gave me a lamb instead.
The lamb to a wise man I took;
The wise man gave me a book.
The book I learned to read.
God has given me what I need.

Afghanistan
(UNICEF Book of Children's Poems)

Whither Thou Goest...

And Ruth said, Intreat me not to leave thee, or to return from following after thee: for whither thou goest, I will go; and where thou lodgest, I will lodge: thy people shall be my people, and thy God my God: Where thou diest, will I die, and there will I be buried: the Lord do so to me, and more also, if ought but death part thee and me.

Ruth 1:16-17

...Nothing goes better with the real spiritual life than mirth. I have a dear friend who tells the story that he and I were once requested to leave a tea shop because of our excessive laughter. We had been discussing with great delight the doctrine of the Trinity, for which both of us had and still have a profound faith and love. And why not? It is rightly said that no one really believes fully in anything until he is prepared to be merry about it. "Him serve with mirth"—that is the right reading.

Both are good things—laughter and the love of friends. And what God has joined together, let no man put asunder. Ever yours, hoping to laugh with you again.

Quintus Quiz

A Family Prayer

Lord Jesus, we would thank Thee that Thou hast blessed our home with the gift of young life, for we know that through our children Thou wouldst remind us of God.

We do resolve, by Thy help, to honor Thee in all our relationships—in our home, so that it may be Thy temple; in our hearts, where Thou dost love to dwell; in our place of business, that it may become an adventure in living our faith.

And now Lord, we place every member of our family in Thy care and keeping. Bless them every one. Be with us all throughout this day...In Jesus' name. Amen.

Peter Marshall

The lasting love of a man and wife is a gift from God.

Author Unknown

The aspiration of lovers: to be as necessary to each other as the world to God, and God to the world.

Richard Garnett

The Garden

What makes a garden?
Flowers, grass and trees,
Fragrance, grace and color:
Lovely gifts like these.

What makes a garden
And why do gardens grow?
Love lives in gardens—
God and lovers know!

Caroline Giltinan

This Is God's World

It is a world filled with knowledge
    and inspiration.
We can find sermons in stone.
There are pathways to follow that lead away
    from self and close to the heart of God.
The wild beasts can teach us nobility
    and courage.
We can learn humility from the violet
    and steadfastness from a star.
And our hearts are filled with joy
    when we realize that we not only live
    in this world God has made,
    but that we are part of His creation.
And as He cares for all His own,
    He cares for us.
As He directs the flight of the smallest
    swallow, He will direct our path,
    and even in the shadowed valleys we need
    fear no evil.
As He arranges the silent stars in harmony
    and beauty, so can He arrange
    the pattern of our lives, helping us create
    order, giving us an inner harmony
    that makes us whole.
As He loves all of His creations, so will He
    love us throughout eternity.

Yes, this is God's world, a world that He has
     fashioned for us; and just as the moon
     reflects the brilliance and splendor of
     the sun, so can our lives reflect the
     power and glory, the joy and beauty of
     God, in whose image we are created.

Dean Walley

Transformation

With the white impersonality of snow
Distinctions are wiped out, and all is beauty.
And it is like this when love rules the heart—
All people seem the same, no matter what
     race or creed;
All shine with the same look: divinity.
When prejudice is ousted, and we love
Without reservation, a change takes place;
We view all mankind as it really is,
Made in His image. And just as the pure
     snow,
God's silver gift, transforms our outer world,
So love transforms our secret inner world,
And hope adds its dazzle, its snow-light,
As hearts, loved, give off their own kind
     of glow.

Pauline Havard

The Light of God

Beyond our power to explain or know,
There is a spark that kindles an inward glow
And turns it outward as a signal fire,
Beaming the farther as it reaches higher.

We need only crack the dark soul's lantern door
And the spark will leap to life at its very core,
Filling the vessel with a blaze of light
And sending a beacon deep into the night.

Lord God, I open my lantern, dark and still.
Kindle my soul with the quick spark of your will.
Let love be my fuel and your truth the flame
That shines out of me to glorify your name.

Barbara Kunz Loots

The God of Love

There is an ocean—cold water without motion. In this ocean, however, is the Gulf Stream, hot water flowing from the equator toward the pole. Inquire of all scientists how it is physically imaginable that a stream of hot water flows between the waters of the ocean, which, so to speak, form its banks, the moving within the motionless, the hot within the cold. No scientist can explain it. Similarly, there is the God of love within the God of the forces of the universe—one with Him, and yet so totally different. We let ourselves be seized and carried away by that vital stream.

Albert Schweitzer

The true meaning of love one's neighbor is not that it is a command from God which we are to fulfill, but that through it and in it we meet God....Existence will remain meaningless for you if you yourself do not penetrate into it with active love and if you do not in this way discover its meaning for yourself. Everything is waiting to be hallowed by you....If you wish to believe, love!

Martin Buber

A Child's Wisdom

One day when I was teaching a Sunday school class of mentally retarded children, I handed out pictures of Jesus which had a rock placed near Him. Then I handed out separate pictures of a tiny boy in a sitting position, thinking that the children could paste him on the rock.

But one little girl promptly pasted him in Jesus' clasped arms.

I often think of the love and trust in this special child's heart that made her see so clearly what many of us never see—that we should always place ourselves in His loving arms. He is our rock.

Lorna Beall

My friends are my estate. Forgive me then the avarice to hoard them! They tell me those who were poor early have different views of gold. I don't know how that is. God is not so wary as we, else He would give us no friends, lest we forget Him! The charms of the heaven in the bush are superseded, I fear, by the heaven in the hand occasionally.

Emily Dickinson

Brothers

Brothers are made to protect
one another.
God made Brothers to be together
and live together.
They are made not to fight. They are
to love one another.
They will grow up and have a house
by each other. Brothers are
for helping one another.

Randy Phillips
(Houston Elementary School)

Of Marriage

Here Love begins to render the prose of Life into hymns and canticles of praise, with music that is set by night, to be sung in the day. Here Love's longing draws back the veil, and illumines the recesses of the heart, creating a happiness that no other happiness can surpass but that of the Soul when she embraces God.

Marriage is the union of two divinities that a third might be born on earth. It is the union of two souls in a strong love for the abolishment of separateness. It is that higher unity which fuses the separate unities within the two spirits. It is the golden ring in a chain whose beginning is a glance, and whose ending is Eternity. It is the pure rain that falls from an unblemished sky to fructify and bless the fields of divine Nature.

As the first glance from the eyes of the beloved is like a seed sown in the human heart, and the first kiss of her lips like a flower upon the branch of the Tree of Life, so the union of two lovers in marriage is like the first fruit of the first flower of that seed.

Kahlil Gibran

A Prudent Wife

The heart of her husband doth safely trust in her, so that he shall have no need of spoil. She will do him good and not evil all the days of her life. She seeketh wool, and flax, and worketh willingly with her hands. She openeth her mouth with wisdom; and in her tongue is the law of kindness. She looketh well to the ways of her household, and eateth not the bread of idleness. Her children arise up, and call her blessed; her husband also, and he praiseth her. *Proverbs 31: 11-13, 26-28*

Love All

Love all God's creation, both the whole and every grain of sand. Love every leaf, every ray of light. Love the animals, love the plants, love each separate thing. If thou love each thing, thou wilt perceive the mystery of God in all; and when once thou perceive this, thou wilt thenceforward grow every day to a fuller understanding of it: until thou come at last to love the whole world with a love that will then be all-embracing and universal.

Fyodor Dostoevski

...We have been told that we must love the Lord God with all our heart and all our soul. But do we love ourself? If we ask ourself this question with all honesty and cast aside all false modesty, our answer should be "Yes." This affirmative answer shows that we love what God has done for us, that is, to make us like Him. That which we love about ourself is really God, and the knowledge of this simple fact can set us free.

Take time to think of what you love about yourself. Our good characteristics are an index of our Godlikeness and our real self. When we express love, we are very much like God, for God is love. All our lovableness, all our loving-kindness is God performing through us. Do we see ourself as sincere, tolerant, peaceable, generous, noble, joyful, helpful? This is God expressing through our humanity.

Mary Jane Henderson

PHOTOGRAPHERS: Dana Bodnar, page 28;
Joan E. Brown, page 25; Guy Burgess, page 12;
Walter Chandoha, page 4; Richard Fanolio,
title page, page 9; Robert Kobrener, page 20;
Sue Morey, pages 17, 45; H. Armstrong Roberts,
page 33; Bill Westerman, page 37; Sam
Zarember, page 40.

Set in Walbaum, a light, open typeface
designed by Justus Erich Walbaum (1768-1839),
who was a typefounder at Goslar and at Weimar.
Printed on Hallmark Crown Royale Book paper.
Designed by Bruce Baker.